Do You Wonder?

To
Max

For
our children
and their families

and

In memory of
my mother, father, and brother

◆

In appreciation to

Russell A. Helms,
editor and book designer,

and

Mary H. Lockhart
for typing the manuscript

Do You Wonder?

SARA MCINTYRE BAHNER

---

47 Journals
PUBLISHING

Copyright © 2014, Sara McIntyre Bahner

All rights reserved.

No part of this book may be reproduced without the author's written consent, except for brief quotations in articles and critical reviews. All rights reserved.

Cover and text design by 47 Journals LLC

Cover image: family table photograph by the author

Printed in the United States

ISBN: 978-0-9786615-8-8

Back cover portrait (oil on canvas) by Eric Johnson, Versailles, Kentucky, 2008

Contents

Introduction	1
Prologue	3
Time	4
October II	5
To Max	6
Basis	7
My Hand	8
Bones	9
Mozart	10
The Gentleness	11
Differences	12
Mortal, Mortal, Mortal Us	13
Contrasts	14
Fleeting Glory	15
A Lovely Time of Year	16
What Does It Matter Now?	17
For Paul L. Reynolds	18
A Child of All Times	19
Pins	20
Parsley	21
The Magnolia Tree	22
Poem for Joy W.	24
A Ploy	25
One Touch	26
The Rhythms	27
Playhouse	28
Janice C.	29
What Is	30
Your Beauties	31
Ode to a Broom	32
Who Knows?	33
The Yearning Time	34
And Walk	35
Dictators Large and Small	36

For Juanita M.	37
Long Poem	38
Small Things	39
Ardent	40
Secondhand Terror	41
Her Own	42
Something	43
See	44
Summoned	45
Label It	46
Hardly Visible	47
Then	48
Our Bank Safe Deposit Box as Microcosm	49
A Measure	50
Hollow House	51
Even If	52
On Waking in the Morning	53
If You Can	54
Elevator Kisses	55
Enough	56
Plastic People	57
From a Picture Book	58
Enjoy	59
The Wake	60
Animals	61
Short Poem	63
Shall We?	64
Voices	65
Night	66
The Well of Your Wanting	67
Overnight Guest at a Friend's House	68
Steps	69
Missy	70
I Am Told	71
At 81	72
Epilogue	73
About the Author	74

Introduction

Sitting under a tall pine tree — a lovely day for studying outside — I could not have known that the poem I wrote there would become the first poem of a book of poems.

I Want

I want whoever I love
to stand and look with me
through tall pine branches
to the sky,
to feel the beauty of green needles
against God's great blue,
and then look down
and smile.

Agnes Scott College
Decatur, Georgia, 1952

Written over many years in many circumstances and locations, these poems tell the story of one family. I have thought poems while standing at the kitchen sink, playing with our children in our yard, or waking in the night, knowing that my husband Max was a steady pleasure and strength.

Put aside in a notebook, the poems accumulated — in pencil and pen on papers large and small, paper-clipped and dated. I realized I could gather them for my family to share joy and thoughts.

My first book, *Autobiography of a Marriage* (2007), is hardback, limited in number, for family and friends. When it was finished, my husband suggested I choose about a third of the poems to be published in paperback. It is called *Chronological Poems* (2007), with a shortened introduction and a new epilogue. I chose, leaving out "Family Sayings," "The Max Poems," and many poems about family members.

That book done, Max encouraged, "Keep writing." Now, with the original introduction amplified, *Do You Wonder?* follows. I hope you wonder.

Prologue

Come Muse, Please

Come Muse, please take my voice and fill
its rhythmic words with beauty till
the sound and sense are one
so passion can enliven it
for gift to those who read.

Each reader must her own voice find
to sing her heart to music's rhyme,
but mine can light her joy perhaps
and start the song she never knew was hers.

June 2, 2005
Norway, North of Hammerfest

Time

Time is a mask
we hide behind.
We need to know
what we want
and what we do not want.

September 1, 2006

October II

The glory that is October
surpasses human pageantry.
    Trees flame in golden light.
    Sky embraces in dearer blue.
    Air invites deep breaths.
    And liveliness is the general condition!

September 16, 2006

To Max

Never, never
will I have his arms around me.
Never, never
will I have his kisses
on my forehead.
Forever, forever
will we have had a life.
Forever, forever
will we have laughed.

September 21, 2006

Basis

What is the basis
of good morals?
The beauty, the desirability
of the good.
What is the basis
of bad morals?
We do not know.

October 11, 2006
on returning from a World War II
battlefield tour in Europe

My Hand

What a marvel
is my hand!
Four soldiers of different heights
standing tall
and a general
at their side
to make men/women of them.

November 22, 2006

Bones

Bones — I saw them —
thousands of bones.
The huge European World War I
monument
has low windows across the back
near the ground.
Thigh bones
were bundled together
like sticks.

January 19, 2007
on returning from a World War II
battlefield tour in Europe

Mozart

Mozart may have
found his music
a great pleasure
to himself,
and, he hoped,
to others.

He may have
touched
the realm of beautiful truth
and could share
because his listeners
had touched it before.

April 22, 2007
Lumberton, North Carolina
The Coterie Weekend

The Gentleness

The gentleness of the leading
is amazing.
When I ask
for teaching,
    tiny adjustment
        by
    tiny adjustment,
I am taught
the direction I may
choose to take.

April 27, 2007

Differences

Why are we so afraid
of differences?
Perceived similarities
may make us feel secure.

I am not white,
I am beige.
You are not black,
you are brown.
So beige and brown
are not
so far apart,
are they?
And it would be fine
if they were far apart,
if we could see.

May 22, 2007
Marion, Alabama

Mortal, Mortal, Mortal Us

Mortal, mortal, mortal us.
How do we get it all done?
How do we see, feel, think, share
before our time is run?

Doing it all is not the point.
Doing it well is the measure.
Richly, richly, richly love
to give the dear world pleasure!

May 23, 2007
Marion, Alabama

Contrasts

I prefer autumn with
contrasts.
Suppose all the yellow trees
stood on one side of the road,
all the red trees
stood on the other,
and the evergreens
declined to stand with either!

November 6, 2007

Fleeting Glory

Fleeting Glory
leaves the hands
of those who try to keep her.
She goes to that unnumbered band
whose hands have sought to help her
      soothe the sick
      and sick of heart,
      bring glad smiles
      to neighbors' eyes
      while calling world the neighbor.
Who know that time
will still their hands
but not the truths
that moved them.

Easter Day 2008
on seeing the grave of
"Mary, Mother of Washington"
Fredericksburg, Virginia

A Lovely Time of Year

A lovely time of year to die.
Picnic tables, bird songs, bright morning sun.
The river Rhine is a good place to be
this June Sunday.

Our cruise takes us past
    towers, churches,
      houses with flower-filled window boxes,
      centuries of castles, vineyards,
      pleasant campgrounds,
      life moving.

Where are the too-young ghosts
who fought here?

June 1, 2008
Germany

What Does It Matter Now?

What does it matter now
that two old silver spoons
on the spoon rack
match
and that they belonged
to a set
from some relative distant in time
who lived and wondered and died
and who left
two silver spoons
with a flower garland
diagonally
across each stem?

July 10, 2008
Home

For Paul L. Reynolds

You have shared
the gift of Music,
wreathed her
in sumptuous flowers.
In flowing gown
and piped to dance
she has led us to
ourselves
and to our loving God.

August 12, 2008
upon his retirement
as Organist/Choirmaster
at St. Paul's Episcopal Church
Chattanooga, Tennessee

A Child of All Times

I would be a
child of all times,
not restricted to
>   one location
>   one language
>   one culture
>   one century.

I would know
what it is
to live,
that I am born
and I die.
What do I do
with the in-between?

October 15, 2008
on returning from Portugal

Pins

Pins — safety and straight —
keys, nails, buttons,
thread and thimbles
left from past generations
tell us,
"We have been here before."

Yes. And now we shall leave
pins — safety and straight —
keys, nails, buttons,
thread and thimbles
to tell the next ones,
"Carry on!"

December 17, 2008
Home

Parsley

My husband and I
went for breakfast
to a new restaurant downtown.

Two eggs over medium,
ham,
wheat bread, butter, jelly,
and grits.

I said to my husband,
"How appealing!
See how much difference
parsley makes?"
I removed it
and looked down
at the now pallid food.

"What is the parsley
in your life?"
I asked him.

January 25, 2009

The Magnolia Tree

Two little girls
in a tall magnolia tree.
Sunshine, expectations.

What would be
even more fun
than sitting
and watching our world?
Lunch — delivered.

Hedgepeth's Pharmacy downtown
served lunches
and also
sent Sip on his bicycle
to deliver them.

We ordered, he came
and put them
in our rope-lowered basket.
How to pay?
Charge ½ to your Daddy,
and I'll charge ½ to mine.

So we ate and laughed
and saw people we knew
in cars or on the sidewalks
and later left notes
for each other
in the water meter hole
next to the street.

Spring 2009
Poem written at Vicki's request. She
lived across the street. What fun!

Poem for Joy W.

How glad we are
that you adorn
our lives.
Smiles abounding
and
laughter reaching
not only to
our hearts
but also to our
histories and futures.
What a gift you have
for sharing life!

March 11, 2009

A Ploy

One
great ploy of Evil
is to help you
hurry
trampling daffodils,
shutting out birds' songs,
gulping time
like fine wine,
missing smiles,
missing tears,
missing life.

March 17, 2009

One Touch

Stonehenge stones
ring me round
only in my memories.
Years ago with husband and children
I walked among
the tall, massive testaments
and was silent
at their grandeur.
I touched
the nearest one
and felt a part
of the people
who had put them there
and of their willing.

Now you cannot walk among the stones.
Protected from too many hands,
they stand near but untouchable,
as they should be,
but I hold my one touch close.

June 20, 2009
Bourton-on-the-Hill,
Moreton in Marsh
Gloucestershire, England

The Rhythms

I like to hear the rhythms.
I like to hear the rhythms.
Do not sing me a lullaby.
Read a poem — because —
I like to hear the rhythms.
    Heart beat.
    Breath beat.
    Feet move, shoulders follow, hands spread.
    Hours, days, months, seasons, years.
    What splendid rhythms!
If nothing else is said of me,
say
"She liked to hear the sweet rhythms."

June 29, 2009
Bourton-on-the-Hill
Moreton in Marsh
Gloucestershire, England

Playhouse

A little girl's playhouse
was in our town cemetery
when I was growing up.
Wooden, white, built over her grave.
Sorely missing her and
visibly grieved,
her parents saw her play no more.

I do not know
when it was removed.
Maybe her parents died, too,
and joined her,
and relatives had it taken down.

July 19, 2009

Janice C.

Smiling, laughing,
enjoying me,
Janice scatters joy
like the sun
scatters sunlight!

August 10, 2009

What Is

I bow before what is.
What is I do not know.
Unless the kindness shows itself,
I have no place to go.

You say,
"It is done,
the Christ-child has come!"
I say,
"I know,
and I love him dearly."
But interpretations can be so sad.
We need to think more clearly.

I come,
arms bare,
to thank the One
who made us and sustains us
even though no thing explains us.

October 22, 2009

Your Beauties

All the beauties
are
yours, mine,
ours.
I may not understand
your language,
but
your music, your architecture, your paintings,
your sculpture, your dance
your kindness to strangers —
I understand your beauties.

November 20, 2009

Ode to a Broom

Leaning against
a back counter
in a fast-food restaurant,
the wood-handled, yellow-strawed broom
seemed to have a
dignity
some people lack.
Worn straw ends showed
"I am needed. I work."

December 10, 2009

Who Knows?

I am not one to wait for heaven.
Who knows?
I am one to watch here
for kindness
scattered like confectioner's sugar
to decorate and sweeten.

Why wait
when joy dances 'round us?
Why sink to despair
when cruelty kills and horror invades
our deeper apprehension?
Because there is deeper yet,
a love beyond all knowing.
Who knows?

December 16, 2009

The Yearning Time

The yearning time
comes quietly
about the first of November.

Other countries,
other centuries,
have known it.
Eden.
Where is Eden?
Why have we lost it?
Did we ever have it?

Yet we know
there must be a place
where the best overcomes the worst
and
children's songs overcome lament.

Shall we yearn forever?

December 21, 2009

And Walk

I have made my peace with
not knowing.
I rest in the
not understood.
I dance my life with
no words
and fall to my knees with
gratitude, joy, anguish, hope,
and walk
among my fellow creatures.

May 12, 2010

Dictators Large and Small

Here I am, World!
You can go home now.
I am in charge,
at least of my own life
and, preferably,
of those in my close circle.

Let us pray for the kindness
of all human beings.

May 15, 2010

For Juanita M.

She has left.
Sweet thing, pretty thing.
So delicate, so kind.

I remember when I met her.
I was a teenager,
and my cousin brought his fiancée
to our beach house
to meet the family.

Their marriage meant
a good life,
three fine children.
In her nineties,
she had long outlived her husband.

This morning, months after,
I again remember her gifts.

August 28, 2010

Long Poem

Time before.
Time after.
You.
Millennia.
Great-great-grandparents.
Great-grandparents.
Grandparents.
Parents.
You.
Children.
Grandchildren.
Great-grandchildren.
Great-great-grandchildren.
Millennia.
Relationships.
Thoughts, feelings.
Speculations?
Distillations.

October 1, 2010

Small Things

Dried leaves, twigs,
a little pinecone,
and a Popsicle stick
are among my treasures.
Given by our four grandchildren
when that was
all they had to give.
Now they make a small arrangement
of memories
in a small, clear bud vase.
Around it
are four cupped shells,
one holding a small stone,
another an acorn.

October 10, 2010

Ardent

The idol of our expectations
is large.
Metal eyes
confront us,
and we bow down.

Ardent devotees of
the good
stand.

March 9, 2011

Secondhand Terror

Secondhand terror
may suffice
for a while
to ward off
firsthand terror
that may be
intolerable.

Is this why
we see movies
and read books
that viscerally frighten?

Many, however, know
firsthand terror
and
have no choice.

March 31, 2011

Her Own

She is her own universe.
She surrounds herself
    with the fairly predictable
    so she has very little adjusting to do.
She has no dealings
    with misery
        or
    the running laughter of children.

She is
    and
        will have been.

June 16, 2011

Something

Something I must bow to.
Something I want to bow to.
Something good.
Something that calls me child.

July 11, 2011

See

A drum beat to the grave
is not what I want.
I want a waltz, a pirouette, a Charleston,
    a liturgical dance, a boogie-woogie!
I want singing — in harmony —
I want a feast of delight
    with family and friends.
I want to say "Thank you!"
    for this one life.

I want to weep
    for other lives
        stunted, painful, hopeless, hungry,
        unloved, thrown away.

I want to shout
    "Wake up world!"
    to see what we do to each other.

August 11, 2011

Summoned

Mortality has summoned me.
I am not loath to go.
Dear ones have gone before
and, though
ones just as dear still live,
I cannot know to tell them
if what I hope
holds true.

October 26, 2011

Label It

How can you stand it, God?
Watching your own dear world
tear itself apart,
your own creation.
Why not just blast it all to oblivion
and label the emptiness
"failed experiment"?

October 28, 2011

Hardly Visible

Gradual evil
is cumulative.
It builds on itself
and is
hardly visible
at first.

December 5, 2011

Then

Then we die.
After what?
Effort.
To roll over, sit up, crawl, stand,
    walk, talk.
Now what?

January 4, 2012

Our Bank Safe Deposit Box as Microcosm

Not the largest
or the smallest,
our bank safe deposit box
is too heavy.
Now that age
has somewhat weakened me,
I have to ask the bank attendant
to set it out.
A coin collection
is the major weight,
but papers are up to the lid inside.
Some things must go.

April 6, 2012

A Measure

Do not disturb the subterranean waters.
Recognize them, respect them, let them flow
for they are not yours, or mainly not,
and you cannot bring them to light
without wounding all concerned.

Maybe someday you can
cup your hands
and draw up a measure
to pour gently, quietly,
where it needs to go
to refresh
those who need to know.

April 15, 2012

Hollow House

Hollow house
filled with tensions.
No joy
of coming or going
passes its doors.

Large rooms
sit empty,
with no lively conversations
or anticipations,
filled with new furniture
like a magazine advertisement
and chosen by
a new wife.

May 14, 2012

Even If

Even if our mortal names
are known
far beyond our time,
the people
who remember them
are mortal, too,
and
they will die.

Far better
than
names known
are gifts shared
and
kindness shown.

June 17, 2012

On Waking in the Morning

Why life?
Why everything?
Why me?

July 15, 2012

If You Can

Sing — dance — scream.
Laugh — despair.
Do not despair.
Say only, if you can,
"I do not know,
    and
I trust."

August 11, 2012

Elevator Kisses

Elevator kisses,
knees touching
under restaurant tables,
hands held on walks in the park,
"Please" and "Thank you"
and "After you"
and "You look so pretty this morning."
Courtesy goes such a long way!

September 3, 2012
New York City

Enough

When is enough enough?
What balance of shape and mass
placed where
in what color, texture,
can quicken the heart
and
begin the smile?

The geometry of heaven
may well be absent,
but I think not.
Delight can come
in many forms,
here and there?

September 7, 2012

Plastic People

Plastic people.
How sad
not to share lives,
not to take pleasure
in others' thoughts.
Unless the eyes
light with mutual discoveries,
what use?

September 7, 2012

From a Picture Book

I am so glad, God,
to sit on this bench
near your throne.

You don't have a throne?
What do you have?

> As your husband's family
> says about secrets,
> "That's for me to know,
> and you to find out!"

Thank you for telling me.
I still want to sit here
and wonder.

September 10, 2012

Enjoy

Do you enjoy being God?
The beautiful gray-on-gray
of morning fog
in winter trees
made me wonder.
What of evil?
We do not know.

January 10, 2013

The Wake

The wake of our ship is very long,
and white foam joins Caribbean blue
to make azure as it stretches behind
and returns to its own color.

Your life can have such beauty,
even if it cannot last.
It joins other people to make
different colors of experience
and returns to its own place,
having brightened its time,
for beauty cannot die.

March 26, 2013
aboard ship in the Caribbean

Animals

We are animals.
We are the worst of animals.
Other animals kill to eat.
(and this is another question)
We kill to kill.*

April 9, 2013

on hearing the BBC World News
*Psalm 8:4 and 5 (Good News Bible, American Bible Society 1976)

"…what is man, that you think of him;
    mere man, that you care for him?
    Yet you made him inferior
      only to yourself*
    You crowned him with glory
      and honor."

*yourself; or the gods, or the angels.

Psalm 8:4 and 5 (New Revised Standard Version, American Bible Society 1989)

"…what are human beings
    that you are mindful of them?
    Yet you have made them
    a little lower than God,*
    and crowned them with
      glory and honor."

* or, the divine beings; or, angels. Hebrew "elohim"

Psalm 8:4 and 5 (The New Oxford Annotated Bible, 3rd edition, New Revised Standard Version, Oxford University Press 2001)

"…what are human beings that you are
    mindful of them,
  mortals that you care for them?
  Yet you have made them a little lower
    than God.*
  And crowned them with glory and
    Honor."

* Humans are endowed with divine glory and honor, perhaps the psalm's equivalent to the human being as "image of God" (Genesis 1:27).

Short Poem

Why try?

Years Ago

Shall We?

The fecund earth.
We came upon it.
Shall we leave it so?

August 15, 2013

Voices

The voices of multitudes
across multi-centuries cry out
in voiceless anguish
for
having been robbed
of their creativity, family, shelter, food.
Tyrants
chose their demise
over sharing power
with unnamed, unnecessary
masses.

September 14, 2013

Night

Night
and Mr. Generous Spirit
lies sleeping by my side.
I lie awake
wondering and thanking for him.
I try not to move too often
so he can rest.

December 17, 2013

The Well of Your Wanting

Guard the well of your wanting —
Desire kindness, truth, beauty, balance,
    accomplishment.
Drink deeply for taste and delight.
Let your joy meet
another's joy
and share the laughter.

December 24, 2013

Overnight Guest at a Friend's House

Very early morning.
Two bird notes at the window.

Why do you think
I made birds sing?
Why do you think
I gave roses
such luscious fragrances
in their spectacular forms?

To delight,
to dance the heart,
to add grace notes.
Sheer gifts
for my Beloveds.

January 12, 2014
Atlanta, Georgia

Steps

Step 1: Banish laughter.
Step 2: Limit sunshine.
Step 3: Outlaw questions.
Step 4: Ration love.
Step 5: Adulterate worship.

    And I, Evil, shall rule
this wretched little planet Earth
   without a fight!

January 15, 2014

Missy

The white at the end
of our Border Collie's black tail
does it for me!
Our Maker
must have a sense of humor
or at least an eye for design.
What glee, what satisfaction!
Other life forms have more intricate patterns,
but white on black,
and wagging in greeting,
does it for me!

March 22, 2014

I Am Told

I am told You love us.
Who is doing the telling?
Other humans who do not know.

Where does the idea originate?
I do not know —
They do not know —
But I hope
    and
I love back.

April 9, 2014

at 81

Into stormy seas sail I
waters dark and waves so high.
I cannot see from foam to foam
to find a course that leads me home.

Unless the One who holds me dear
boards my ship and helps me steer,
I cannot sail the oceans wide
that means she lived before she died.

Yet trust I now
and trust I then
the One to come
as friend with friend
since I have never known the why
of life here now
or life so nigh.

July 7, 2014

Epilogue

On Poetry

She has come again!
Pay heed.
Take the first line.
It is the thought
to hold the rest.
Follow the dance,
for she moves quickly
and does not come again
for a season.
What joy to follow her lead
to flower strewn fields,
glad or sad,
with only the celebration of writing.

September 15, 2013

About the Author

Sara Minta McIntyre Bahner was born and reared in Lumberton, North Carolina, the only daughter of Clara Margaret Pope and Robert Allen McIntyre and sister of Robert, Jr. She attended Agnes Scott College in Decatur, Georgia, for two years and graduated Phi Beta Kappa and *summa cum laude* from Wake Forest College, concentrating in sociology and philosophy.

She is married to Thomas Maxfield Bahner, who practices law in Chattanooga, Tennessee. They have borne four children and buried two. She and her husband share interests in books, music, theology, cooking, travel, friends, and home. Her particular delights are family, liturgical dance, writing poetry, singing, and investing.

"I considered long before I included the college honors. Since I have not had a named profession, I wanted to show some basis for thought and expression."

~ S.M.B.

www.ingramcontent.com/pod-product-compliance
Lightning Source LLC
Chambersburg PA
CBHW030448300426
44112CB00009B/1221